TH(

V1

Best Wishes
From James T. Wray.

THOUGHTS IN VERSE

by

James T. Wray

First published by
James T. Wray
1999

Copyright © James T. Wray 1999

All rights reserved. No part of this publication may be reproduced or transmitted in any form or by any means, electronic, mechanical, photocopying, recording or in any information or retrieval system, without the prior permission from the author.

Typeset in Plantin

ISBN 0 9535252 0 1

Printed by
N. Murphy Printing, 7 Lower Crescent, Belfast BT7 1NR

FOREWORD

I think as you read this book you will find the title self explanatory. Quite a few poems will give you an insight to my thoughts as both man and boy. I think most of us like to look back on our childhood days, you will see by the contents of this book that I am no exception. You will no doubt notice I like to write about my dear village Caledon which is never far from my thoughts. Many things have disappeared from my village, so I thought poetry would be one way to let future generations know about the history of their village and to keep it to mind. They will never have the same chance as we had to see our famous 'Woollen Mill' the 'Falls' the 'Mill Race' the 'Soldiers Huts' or to see the Clogher Valley train chug down the middle of our main street, these were all part of Caledon's history and helped to fill our minds with beautiful thoughts. I will mention too some of my close friends I enjoyed as man and boy. I personally look upon all Caledonians as my friends, like I have said before I love my village, but a village can only be as good as the people in it. I also try my hand at humour, you will quickly see I have a rather warped sense of humour. I am not a literary person, so I hope you will bear with me. The absence of this skill makes it hard for me to express all that I'd like to say, and yet I feel quite pleased with my book, I think as you read it, it will tell you all that I wanted to say. So read on and see if some of my poems revive some pleasant childhood memories of your own. I hope you enjoy the contents of this book, for this is just my way of trying to give pleasure to all who enjoy the poetic word.

JAMES T. WRAY

DEDICATIONS

I dedicate this book to the memory of my former teacher Miss Mary O'Neill from Aughnacloy who taught the sons and daughters of Caledon for many generations. I would also like to dedicate this book to my Grandmother Mrs. Rose Hughes and my Wife Kathleen Wray. Without any of these ladies there would be nothing.

****

A special dedication to my sons Jim and John and also to my daughter in law Brigid and my grandchildren who have given me so much happiness.

****

THE COVER — Once again I am indebted to a very talented lady (I can't seem to get away from them, thank goodness) The Cover was designed by Frances Barrett, who runs a very useful business called 'Barprint'.

INTRODUCTION

Jim Wray has capitulated at last. For many years, Jim a prolific producer of verse, Has resisted taking the advice of his friends and admirers and has stubbornly refused to go into print. That is all in the past now, and the first of what I hope will be many books, is in circulation. You may well ask, What sort of a poet is Jim? What subjects does he write about? Many would say he is a narrative poet and they would be partly right. Others venture the opinion that writing about nature is his forte, and they would not be wrong, but I don't think he has been converted to pantheism. A mystic? A philosopher? A thespian? A theologian? I tell the truth, Jim Wray is a glorious mixture of all those I mentioned.

We often hear of men being born before their time, but here is a poet born after his time. Had Jim lived nearer to the era when Ireland was a land of saints and scholars he would indeed have held an exaulted post in the palaces of kings because of his special gift with his pen, or should I say quill? The story teller, the bard, was a person set apart, because he was the media of the day. Can you imagine one person today clever enough, competent enough to be newspaper editor, radio and television director, and possessing the time and the talent to play an active role on internet. As I say, Had Jim walked this earth years ago, his would have been a job of great importance and responsibility, and well equipped he would have been to fulfill his duties.

Besides, Jim has the gift to see The Saviour's "Blood upon the roses" to see in the stars "The glory of his eyes" He can contemplate a grain of sand and picture the shifting whispering sands of the vast desert. In a single drop of water he can visualise the miles and miles of heaving ocean. Jim can pick up the cry of a hungry infant and magnify it so that we can hear and be moved by the mighty cry of hunger coming from the third world. Such is the gift that this poet possesses. You will read this book of poems and find much to appeal to you personally, and you will long for more. The good news is this, as Jimmy Crickett would say beckoning you forward with a flick of his fingers "Come here, there's more".

Joseph Sheehan

ACKNOWLEDGEMENTS

The first people I would have to thank would be my Grandfather John Henry Hughes and my Grandmother Rose Hughes. I lived with them during my first childhood days in Caledon. It was they who encouraged me to learn to read and write by helping me with my homework duties. They showed such patienoe (Especially My Grandmother) and they needed it all. I thank my father James Wray (Jimmy) and my mother Mary Wray (nee Hughes) for the life they gave me. I have to offer a great vote of thanks to two very dear friends of mine in Patsy Sherry from the famous townland of Aughnasallagh and Joe Sheehan from Dungannon. They were the first people who encouraged me to go public with my poems. Patsy gave me openings at any concert that he ran, which lead to appearances elsewhere. Joe who was the headmaster at Saint Mary's School at Cabragh and he in turn helped my confidence by asking me to talk to the pupils of his school about my thoughts on poetry. I dare not leave out Eilish and Kathleen my friends respective wives, they were always there when needed. One person to whom I owe a great debt of thanks is my former teacher Miss Mary O'Neill from Aughnacloy who taught me practically everything I know. Without her skills this book would never have happened. I hope my efforts please her as she looks down on me from her great reward in Heaven. I would also have to offer my humble thanks to that great literary man from Glasslough in the person of Sir Shane Leslie. He gave me wonderful praise and encouragement when he read my poems while making his periodic visit to my school in Caledon, that was in the year of 1949. He rewarded me with the sum of five Shillings(25p) I am just sorry I ever spent it. Now I come to the person who has helped me in more ways than I would have time to write about. That of course is my dear wife Kathleen. She offered encouragement during my darkest time and made me believe in myself. Not only that, she tended to most of the menial tasks that need doing when one undertakes a project like this book. I will not dare to say that I am a great man but one thing I am sure of "Behind me there was a great woman" This acknowledgement shows the number of women who helped to guide and shape my life. I have been a very fortunate man to have such a strong force behind me.I only hope I have managed to do them justice with this book 'Thoughts In Verse'.

JAMES T. WRAY

CONTENTS

MY LESSON FROM LIFE	11
THE END OF AN ERA	13
CONSERVATION	15
TO BE A FRIEND	16
CALEDON OF YESTERYEAR	17
SWEET TYRONE	20
MY NIGHT WITH A FLEA	22
THE CLINGING MIST	23
AN EXILE'S THOUGHTS OF HOME	24
RECOLLECTIONS OF THE FALLS	26
THE VISITOR'S LAMENT	28
THE PHOTOGRAPH	30
MY C.V.	31
ENCOUNTERS WITH THE PAST	32
ADVICE	34
THE HAT	35
A VISIT TO THE DENTIST	36
MOTHER NATURE	38
LOVE'S MESSAGE	40
INVISIBLE FRIEND	41
DREAMS OF HOME	42
A REMINDER TO THE HUMAN RACE	44
MY NANCY	46
THOUGHTS OF CHILDHOOD	48
LET'S	50
A MOTHER	52
NO RETURN	54
THOUGHTS	55
THE CALEDON OF OLD	56
HEAVEN'S GATE	59
THANKING GOD	61
NOT SO BLIND	63
THE OLD RED BRAE	65
FEATHERED FRIENDS	67
CHRISTMAS THOUGHTS	68
SANTA	69
A TREE'S VIEWPOINT	70

FUTILITY	71
A HOPE	72
GREATNESS	73
DIANA	74
OLD COINS	75
THE OLD STONE BRIDGE	76
LIFE'S DREAM	78
LAST THOUGHTS	79
SUBTLETY	80
MORNING BLISS	81
WISHFUL THINKING	82
THE LONG WEEK	83
SORROW IS PEACE	84
THE MASTER GARDENER	85
MY WIFE IS MY LIFE	87
AN ARMCHAIR VIEW	89
THE CLOGHER VALLEY TRAIN	90
THE CHANCE	91
LONELINESS	93
PLEASE RETURN	95
THE LUCK OF FRIENDSHIP	97
THE FRAUD	99
DEAR DESCENDANTS	100
WRITING	102

MY LESSON FROM LIFE
A dedication to my dear teacher Miss Mary O'Neill

As I look on my younger days,
And I look at the bygone scene,
I wonder if I'd changed my ways,
Would I have reigned supreme.

As a boy of five when I started school,
And knew little of the world,
I little thought of the wicked place,
To where my person had unfurled.

To me it was a great big game,
Full of fun for girls and boys,
I thought it would always be the same,
Full of sweets and toys.

But soon my life began to change,
From the things I first had thought,
To me it seemed so very strange,
When knowledge was what I sought.

I did not seek it hard enough,
I did not attend my school,
But soon I felt it rather rough,
To be made to feel a fool.

I met my teacher Miss O'Neill,
When at the age of ten,
A little better I started to feel,
As I picked up all the gen.

She worked so very hard with me,
She taught me all she could,
I never met anyone quite like she,
For she was so kind and good.

She was the Shepherd and I the lamb,
We worked with might and main,
I worked so hard to pass an exam,
While she had held the rein.

We did well in that three years,
But soon I grew so tired,
And realised my early fears,
My want for knowledge had expired.

So the time came when I had to face,
A world so very rough,
I knew as I took my place,
My knowledge was not enough.

So I must do the menial task,
And face the world with fears,
And hide behind a cheerful mask,
And think of those early lost years.

To all of you who hear this rhyme,
Don't do the same as me,
Go to school all the time,
And your knowledge will set you free.

THE END OF AN ERA
The river drainage scheme, a desecration of God's work.

The old bridge, the falls and the Mill Race have gone,
How I wish they could have stayed,
And so too has 'The Sandbeds'
Where once we all had played.

No more is there a 'Mud Hole'
'The Big Sally's' gone as well,
Just how much we'll miss them,
It's very hard to tell.

'The Eighth Field Sandbeds' have vanished,
And bless me Oh' my Lord,
They've done away with the 'Broken Bank'
And 'Dan McKenna's Ford'

They've cut away the corners,
To change the river's course,
Did they think this helpful,
I'm sure it's for the worse.

They say it's for a good cause,
To let the water flow away,
But surely it was time enough,
For it to reach Lough Neagh.

No longer is there an 'Island Holm'
Its completion was made by a ridge,
And the river it seems to be pining,
Since they moved 'The Metal Bridge '

I wonder what it all achieves,
To whom should we offer thanks,
That because of all these changes,
No more can we walk her banks.

They've cut down all the trees,
I'm really lost for words,
I know that I shall miss them,
And so too will the birds.

I know the river will still be there,
But never again the same,
I know it's still 'The Blackwater'
But it's only there in name.

They have made the river straighter,
So the water will run fast,
Yet all they have achieved for me,
Is to cut away my past.

So to the men who did this deed,
I will not bear them malice,
I will offer all to penance,
And take up my heavy chalice.

I will never agree to all these changes,
I think they're a holy terra,
Because as far as I'm concerned,
It's simply 'The End Of An Era'

CONSERVATION

When Winter comes and cold winds blow,
I love to sit by my fire's glow,
I oft do curl up on my seat,
To feel all snug at my fire's heat,

But if the heat is given by coal,
In the ground I see a hole,
And if it's wood that's heating me,
The life's been taken from a tree.

If I'm warmed by glowing peat,
Cut to the shape of logs,
A horrid picture comes to mind,
I see the shrinking of our bogs.

And if my heat it comes from oil,
Which was stored beneath Earth's soil,
Still my heart is full of fears,
To put it there took a million years.

But just before my heart it sank,
I try to make my mind go blank,
For I too do like the best,
So my conscience I will not test.

So I sit at my fire brave and bold,
Anything's better than the feel of cold,
So you see,
That's the type of me,
I keep warm with electricity,
It's not as bad as an open fire,
For all the heat comes down a wire.

TO BE A FRIEND

If you wish to be a friend,
It's so easy for to do,
Just simply do to others,
As you'd like it done to you.

Let's not be dishonest,
Let's do what good we can,
Look not for the faults,
But the good in every man.

Let not our tongues speak evil,
Keep good thoughts in your mind,
Let's not do a cruel act,
Be good and true and kind.

Let's try to love our fellow man,
And do what is their will,
Tend to them in good times,
Don't wait until they're ill.

Let honesty be your policy,
It will pay off in the end,
We'll always put our trust,
In those who are a friend.

So fear not to place your trust,
And your kindred spirits bind,
For a true friend is very rare,
And so very hard to find.

CALEDON OF YESTERYEAR
(1948-1950)

As I look back on my boyhood days,
And the mists of time stand still,
I see Caledon as it used to be,
A village so full of goodwill.

It seems like only yesterday,
The streets were full of children playing,
Be it hide and seek, or scourging hoops,
Or on the 'Tanyard' sleighing.

As I stepped out in the morning,
For my start to another day,
I was greeted by the golden Sun,
As it rose from Killylea.

Still I see the cobbled Church-Hill,
With half-doored houses on each side,
As it swept down to the Main street,
A street so long and wide.

In our village there was an Englishman,
We're glad 'twas ours he chose,
For he had a little cafe shop,
His name was Frederick Rose.

After Frederick left this shop,
Came a man of great renown,
He ran the shop with a room for darts,
His name was big Jack Brown.

Willie Ramsey was a Cobbler,
Who lived on the Castle Lane,
He served us well for many a year,
Till his eyesight it did wane.

But Willie he had a rival,
Whose skill brought equal fame,
He lived upon the old Church-Hill,
Mervyn Noble was his name.

Harry McMullan was a tailor,
He lived at the Corner Bar,
His skill with thread a needle,
Was known both near and far.

Joe Hughes from Mill Street fixed our clocks,
Sometimes he cut our hair,
No matter what we needed,
In Caledon we had it there.

There was Campbell's shop and Dickson's,
To our eyes they brought a gleam,
'Twas here we used to congregate,
To buy sweets, or lick ice cream.

I recall there were lots of grocery shops,
They supplied us with lots of food,
Harriett Mercer's Christmas window,
Made sure to where our eyes were glued.

Jane McKenna had a drapery shop,
Mr. Knox practiced a butcher's trade,
There was the Corner Bar, beside the 'Big Tree'
Where many a plan was made.

Jimmy Allen owned a hardware shop,
He sold tools with which to toil,
Still I see Tommy Drennan's yard,
Where we bought our paraffin oil.

Charlie Mercer supplied us with petrol,
Many a puncture I know he did mend,
And the punctures weren't always in wheels,
To our footballs he often did tend.

'Wee Mercer's', was the place for comics,
It's a shop I remember so well,
They were grocers as well as newsagents,
How they coped I really can't tell.

Jim Rolston ran an electrical shop,
There was a pub 'The Caledon Inn'
Caledon United was our football team,
How we hoped they would always win.

There was George McGloughlin's the Chemist,
Scott Bros for groceries and coal,
Alec Robinson too owned a grocery store,
He too played a vital role.

I know that there were other shops,
That are missing from this rhyme,
Like McVeigh's, Stewart's and 'Old Ma Farl's'
But they were before my time.

We also had a Court House,
Just under 'The Old Town Clock'
Where many a man and woman trembled,
When summoned to stand in the dock.

Still I see that 'Old Town Clock'
On its time we could all rely,
It now stands still and silent,
As if time had passed it by.

What stories that clock could tell us,
Of the years as it stood on high,
How it gave its time to the passengers,
As the Clogher Valley train chugged by.

In those days the people were happy,
Its a thought that makes me glad,
I'm happy they know not of the changes,
For they might have made them sad.

And now that all this time has passed,
And I know it's caught up with me,
I still see the Caledon of old,
It's all here, in my memory.

SWEET TYRONE

Of all the places in this world,
That I would love to own,
It's a little bit of Ireland,
Called the County of Tyrone.

For in this County lies a village,
The one I love the best,
It's here I'll always want to stay,
When I am laid to rest.

I speak of dear old Caledon,
Where I'll live until I die,
It lies in the Clogher Valley,
The Blackwater flows nearby.

It's the birthplace of Alexander,
Her famous soldier son,
He fought for victory at Alamein,
We know of course he won.

It's Tyrone among the bushes,
It's the home of the clan O'Neill,
Yet when I see the Sperrin's,
It's my heartbeat that I feel.

Its countryside has rugged beauty,
With whins on hills and brae,
Yet still I see her border,
As it reaches to Lough Neagh.

I picture all her waterways,
Be it river, bog or lake,
I wish I was a painter,
What a picture I could make,

I'd paint the fields of fresh green crops,
Some with hay new mown,
I'd paint the splendid golden Sun,
As it set o'er sweet Tyrone.

I would capture all her countryside,
With its beauty so serene,
I'd also paint her stately trees,
With their forty shades of green.

I'd picture all her valleys,
In the shrouded morning mist,
Tinted by the rising Sun,
A scene that God has kissed.

I think of those who in the past,
Had fought for what was good,
And died upon a foreign shore,
For they had spilled their blood.

Yet when they got to Heaven,
They'd feel they were at home,
For in that place of splendour,
Sure it looked like sweet Tyrone.

I think too of her people,
Who made this place their home,
And others who like myself,
For work they had to roam.

Yet when I think of lovely Ireland,
With that beauty of its own,
I only think of one dear spot,
The County of Sweet Tyrone.

MY NIGHT WITH A FLEA

A terrible thing happened one night to me,
As I hopped in to bed with a big buck flea,
It bit my toe and it bit my heel,
So very itchy I started to feel.

But my pulse it really started to race,
As it started to bite in a private place,
I scratched around and did my best,
But the blighter went and bit my chest.

He bit my arm and gave my tum a peck,
The next thing I knew he was at my neck,
He pinched my ears and I thought here goes,
And sure enough he bit my nose.

He must have felt at home on me,
But he hadn't heard of D.D.T.
So that fateful night, I gave him a spray,
The funeral's at twelve on Saturday.

THE CLINGING MIST

It creeps so eerily o'er the ground,
Each blade of grass is kissed,
It creeps along with ne'er a sound,
That shrouded thing called mist.

It whirls around so swiftly,
When the wind decides to blow,
For it ... there is no hurry,
For it has nowhere to go.

Sometimes it hangs so still and silent,
Its mystery it never yields,
Its cloak does make all things alike,
As it spreads o'er towns and fields.

That clinging shroud of whiteness,
Sometimes sways too and fro,
It's only from a bright light,
That we may see a glow.

How it loves to paint those pictures,
When it meets its friend Jack Frost,
Its beauty can be treacherous,
Yet we never count the cost.

The Sun and wind come to our aid,
That mist has gone again,
Its left us with its pictures,
On webs and window pane.

Goodbye for now Oh' clinging Mist,
Goodbye my eerie friend,
I'll see you in the Autumn,
Its then you set your trend.

AN EXILE'S THOUGHTS OF HOME

On the day I left dear Ireland,
I was in a state of shock,
As I stood upon the Ferry boat,
And my parents upon the dock.

I knew the way they really felt,
Though they tried to show no sign,
Yet my emotions they flooded out,
With the rendering of Auld Lang Syne.

As the ferry boat made its way to sea,
I had many things on my mind,
My thoughts they lay in a country home,
To the girl I'd left behind.

I was on my way to England,
A journey I faced with dread,
Yet I had to make my fortune,
For the time when I would wed.

Soon I arrived in England,
'Twas strange on that foreign shore,
But this was the place for employment,
And I was a man who was poor.

I was pleased to work on the railway,
Opportunities I know they were scant,
I was lucky too with my lodgings,
I stayed with my favourite Aunt.

My job it gave me time to think,
And my thoughts they oft did roam,
To that quaint little village Caledon,
The place I knew as home.

I'd walk the tracks in the evening time,
It's then my thoughts would switch,
To my friends at Dickson's window,
Or to those on the football pitch.

Everything seemed so clear to me,
Though my heart would ache with pain,
I'd picture a Social in the old 'Hib. Hall'
Which lay in the Castle Lane.

Boys and girls would walk the street,
Just to pass the time of day,
I knew they'd pass my parents home,
If they walked to the old 'Red Brae'

Though my thoughts would oft be with them,
I wondered if they thought of me,
As they gathered around 'The Fountain'
Or stood at the old 'Big Tree'

I'd picture Caledon as the evening set,
'Twas a time that I did like,
And I thought if I listened hard enough,
The town clock I'd hear it strike.

I'd see the houses on the old lough road,
Which I passed as I went to school,
Still I'd see that empty forge,
Where a blacksmith once did rule.

When the time came for my return,
To my village in the glade,
My heart did ache with pain once more,
To see the changes they had made.

RECOLLECTIONS OF THE FALLS

As I stand here on the new road bridge,
Which, joins Armagh to the County Tyrone,
Many thoughts do crowd my mind,
As I stand here all alone.

My mind travels back many years ago,
People crowd on the Armagh bank,
This is where their Summer was spent,
No matter what creed or rank.

Still I see those smiling faces,
What memories my mind recalls,
As they sat in blissful contentment,
By those rippling 'Water Falls'

'The Falls' it formed our swimming pool,
As the water reached up to its brim,
It's here the girls and boys of my youth,
Splashed around and learned how to swim.

We'd swim from 'The Falls' to the bridge,
In those waters that looked so serene,
No-one felt their health at risk,
In those days the water was clean.

Below 'The Falls' in the rippling waters,
Anglers would be wading about,
With a swishing rod they'd cast a fly,
For to lure that crafty Trout.

Still I see boys netting Gudgeon,
'Twas a sport we all did like,
They'd peel the bark from an Ash plant,
To catch minnows as bait for Pike.

This part was known as 'The Sandbeds'
Where the water was not so deep,
Parents could let their children play,
As through the shallows they'd creep.

Suddenly my mind returns to the present,
And a tear it swells in my eye,
Is this the river of my dreams,
As I watch the shallow waters flow by.

I think back to those joyful faces,
How sad they would look to-day,
For they little thought in those golden days,
That 'The Falls' could be taken away.

I know this river is the one in my dream,
But where did all the water go,
For this is not the river I knew,
Or loved all those years ago.

I wish I'd lived in another age,
Maybe a hundred or two years ago,
I could then have spent my lifetime,
Watching those 'Water Falls' flow.

But the good Lord had other plans,
To put me here... to make this my home,
So that I could see it all,
And record it all here in this poem.

If that is his wish then I'm happy,
I will try to do his will,
Yet I'm glad he left me my memory,
For 'The Falls' I can see them still.

THE VISITOR'S LAMENT

In recent times we've had many inventions,
We're all affected in some little way,
There's one I think which affects us most,
I'll explain to you if I may.

I well remember... how in days long gone,
We'd call on our neighbour for a chat,
We'd spin our yarns and tell our jokes,
And talk about this and that.

That is not the case these days,
All talk is out for a start,
We have to sit in stoney silence,
Conversation's become a lost art.

These days there is a lock on the door,
I recall when this door was open,
To-day one knocks for an answer,
The response you feel is a token.

They might say "Come on in,
But go as easy as you can go,
We're all very busy at the moment,
For we're watching a T.V. show."

I enter the room... some people might nod,
As I search for an empty seat,
I might say "It's a grand day"
But my silence I'm told to keep.

So I sit down with the rest of them,
Though I wonder just what is the point,
As I sit there... afraid to move,
For they might hear a creak from my joint.

I try to think of happier days,
When all they wanted was me,
And not to be like a statue,
Staring at an old T.V.

Sometimes I sit for a longsome hour,
My thoughts they start to roam,
What made me pay this visit,
I could have watched the T.V. at home.

During commercials I try to speak,
But I have to speak with great haste,
Commercials they last three minutes or so,
So there's not a second to waste.

Sometimes I wonder about my fate,
Are they channelled to the B.B.C.
If that's the case... I've had it,
I doubt if they'll notice me.

After a time the T.V. will end,
For hours it kept their eyes glued,
It's then they'll say "We're glad to see you,
I hope you don't think that we're rude"

I sit and stare... what can I say,
After all it's their own affair,
Yet still I pose the question,
How come their eyes are not square.

T.V. Can be a very fine thing,
Of that there's little doubt,
Yet still I find it very sad,
When it shuts your neighbours out.

It gives you all the worldly news,
But this I have to say,
T.V. may bring the world to you,
But your friends are kept away.

I too own a T.V. set,
But I do the friendly job,
When a neighbour or friend... enters my home,
I reach for the switch off knob.

THE PHOTOGRAPH

One day I saw a photograph,
All placed upon a mount,
I saw a face so wrinkled,
That they were hard to count.

I saw his eyes were cross-eyed,
His nose hung like a beak,
His face it was so dirty,
To clean would take a week.

I showed it to some others,
They said it can't be bad,
They thought it was a picture,
Of my dear departed dad.

I showed it to another friend,
To see what he could see,
'Twas then I got a terrible shock,
When he said it looked like me.

MY C.V.

When e'er I go to seek a job,
It seems so strange to me,
They seek the words of others,
They'll ask for my C.V.

How come they will not trust me,
Why can't they take my word,
Yet I'm the one they seek,
To me it seems absurd.

They take the word of others,
Yet mine isn't good enough,
Why do they interview me,
Why let me strut my stuff.

They'll place their trust in my C.V.
It's so important to them,
And yet it may not tell the truth,
I could be useless... or a gem.

How come they'll read my old C.V.
And they'll heed what it does say,
Though it may be written by people,
Who wouldn't bid them time of day.

If you wish to use my efforts,
Just look me in the eye,
I don't claim to be the best,
All I can do is try.

ENCOUNTERS WITH THE PAST

As I look around my village Caledon,
And I see the wondrous scene,
With trees of majestic splendour,
And the fields of verdure green.

We are part of the Clogher Valley,
The Blackwater flows nearby,
It's the only place I want to rest,
When it comes my turn to die.

I've listened to the old folks,
Their voices I hear them still,
As they spoke of times of plenty,
With work at the old 'Woollen Mill'

The Mill made many families stay,
For they were a hard working folk,
They plied their trade of weaving,
As the chimney belched out its smoke,

To-day the Mill has vanished,
It too had its strife and trouble,
The Big Chimney too has gone,
Like the Mill it was turned into rubble.

'The Old Mill Theatre' was part of the Mill,
Which held many a dance so grand,
Oh' how we loved to shake a leg,
To Joe Gillespie's band.

There was the old road down to the Gate Lodge,
By 'Charlies Orchard' and the 'Soldiers Huts',
These landmarks too have vanished,
With no question of ifs and buts.

For in these huts many a concert was held,
Local talent would supply the treat,
The eager folk filed in each night,
There was never an empty seat.

Caledon Hill supplied the village with food,
Red deer roamed the vast Demesne,
This was the home of Earl Alexander,
Who fought for victory at El Alamein.

Many sons and daughters did leave us,
To find work they had to roam,
But come October... the Red Deer would roar,
As if to call them all back home.

Many did return with their fortunes made,
Back to this village grand,
Others I know... would like to have come,
But they died on a foreign land.

So to-day as I look up our Main Street,
I see ghosts but I have no fear,
For I see them as they used to be,
They are friends of yesteryear.

What do they think of the old place now,
Do they think our actions insane,
As they search for homes, long gone,
On the Church Hill and Castle lane.

They look long and hard at the new Church Hall,
As around 'The Fountain' they drool,
For in their young days of learning,
It was known as 'The Infant School'

They look amazed at new dwellings,
As they head for the famous 'Big Tree'
Here too I see why they're puzzled,
It's not as big as it used to be.

They look at me lost and forlorn,
Their eyes are filled with pain,
I hope they don't ask me questions,
For these changes I couldn't explain.

ADVICE

Most people pray to go to Heaven,
It's the place they want to go,
But it could be, your friends to see,
You'd need to go down below.

So be careful who you pick as friends,
Please listen to my voice,
For if you wait, and leave it late,
You may not have a choice.

So if your company is very bad,
And you can't stand the heat of fire,
Tell them so... that you can't go,
But you'll send them down a wire.

THE HAT

An old man he lay dreaming,
As he stretched upon his bed,
He dreamt he went to Heaven,
With his hat upon his head.

Saint Peter met him at The Gate,
Says he I tell to you,
To wear a hat that looks like that,
I dare not let you through.

Don't judge by my appearance,
Is what the old man said,
Judge me by my deeds,
And not what's on my head.

The old man turned to Peter,
His pride all hurt and torn,
He mentioned about the Master's Hat,
For it was made from thorn.

Saint Peter sat and thought a while,
For he knew these words were true,
So he opened up the Gate,
And he let the old man through.

A VISIT TO THE DENTIST

We've all suffered that terrible pain,
It's as much as we can take,
We'll take all sorts of potions,
To get rid of that dreaded toothache.

As the morning arrives and also the pain,
What to do I don't seem to know,
It's then I pluck up my courage,
And off to the Dentist I go.

I arrive at the Dentist's surgery,
There's a receptionist so prim and neat,
Then come the words to start my ordeal,
I'm asked to please take a seat.

I enter the room and sit down,
There are others in much the same state,
We sit and stare at each other,
We wonder just what is our fate.

Out of date magazines I try to read,
As the receptionist calls out to me,
I'm told in a very plaintive tone,
To make my way to room three.

I make my way to the room with foreboding,
I enter and sit on the chair,
I look around at the tools of the trade,
Then lie back and wait in despair.

I'm told to lie back and not worry,
By the Dentist who stands at my side,
He then puts on my dark glasses,
And my mouth he then opens it wide.

Suddenly he touches the offender,
I try to hold back a shout,
I'm told my tooth is very bad,
I'm told it must come out.

He steps forward, syringe in hand,
And the needle it enters my gum,
Soon my worries they drift away,
As my mouth it starts to feel numb.

I'm told to lie back and be brave,
To obey I do my best,
There was little else that I could do,
For he had his knee on my chest.

With a sudden jerk the tooth is out,
I'm glad the job it's been done,
I'm told it's just the beginning,
For he says he's pulled the wrong one.

He looks inside my mouth once more,
I think he's about to poke,
I'm then told to rinse my mouth,
I'm told it's only a joke.

I nod my head to show relief,
I couldn't answer, my mouth was so numb,
After all, why should I care,
The offender was gone from my gum.

I mumble my thanks for a job well done,
From the surgery I start to creep,
Now I can smile and feel so brave,
For to-night I know I will sleep.

MOTHER NATURE

Mother Nature moves with gentle grace,
She works the whole year round,
She keeps a smile upon her face,
As she toils with earthly ground.

Her first Season is happiest of all,
To her face a smile it does bring,
It is the Season of awakening,
The Season we know as Spring.

Up will shoot the bulbous plants,
Fields turn to verdure green,
Leaves unfold to clothe the trees,
Birds do sing and feathers preen.

Flowers bloom to give us colour,
Birds work to build their nest,
The world it seems at peace,
Mother Nature has done her best.

Farmers plough and sow their crops,
For them there's little sleep,
Mother Nature needs a helping hand,
Till the crops are ripened to reap.

Each Season it passes so quickly,
Mother Nature has no time to rest,
She must prepare for the Summer,
She wants to look at her best.

Summer will answer many questions,
How come we had all those showers,
The answer lies in her wondrous trees,
And the spread of her profuse flowers.

Young birds leave their cosy nest,
As they fly to swoop and dive,
They fill our ears with music,
They help keep our hearts alive.

The scene is set for those Summer walks,
Mother Nature... what thanks can we give her,
As we stroll along a country lane,
Or the banks of a long winding river.

It's here we see her artful work,
The result for which she did thrive,
As aquatic plants sway too and fro,
'Tis the river's flow that makes them alive.

Its surface is covered with countless flies,
We wonder why they are about,
A plumping sound brings the answer,
They're a meal for the hungry Trout.

Soon this Summer scene must change,
Mother Nature, her heart's in dread,
As she takes away the verdure green,
And the flowers they die in their bed.

As Autumn draws near, she starts to fear,
With the falling of the crumpled leaves,
As the trees hold up their bare arms,
As if they'd just rolled up their sleeves.

This Season makes for gradual change,
From the beauty which gave us delight,
It prepares us for those Winter ills,
When the scene will all turn to white.

This Season too has its beauty,
It's time for a different show,
As we change to crispy brightness,
Caused by the ice and the snow.

Mother Nature still moves with gentle grace,
What changes her movements bring,
Still that smile is upon her face,
As she works to bring us our Spring.

LOVE'S MESSAGE

The young man reached to gain a touch,
To reach the girl he loved so much,
He reached to kiss to seek her taste,
Soon his arms were round her waist.

He felt at ease... she liked it too,
It seemed the natural thing to do,
She felt so safe from care and strife,
This loving man... she'd be his wife.

This is the way it was meant to be,
If all the people could only see,
The greatest gift we have is love,
A gift we gained from God above.

So please no evil, greed or war,
That is not what we are for,
We are here to fill this life,
With all that's good and see off strife.

Let's do good... don't judge in haste,
Remember those arms around the waist,
And if you think God asks too much,
Please remember that couples touch.

INVISIBLE FRIEND

I may be lonely, but never alone,
Please don't think I'm on my own,
For there is someone you can't see,
Who is always standing there with me.

I hope his love I never loss,
He died for me upon that cross,
He makes sure I'm not alone,
Since for my sins he did atone.

I will always be his friend,
To justify his painful end,
For when I sin, my heart goes pale,
I see his hands and feet with nail.

Should my patience e'er be worn,
I see his head crowned with thorn,
And should my loyalty e'er be slack,
I see the lash marks on his back.

For me... this man he had to die,
The least that I can do is try,
To be a trusting worthy friend,
And do the things he did intend.

Then both of us have lots to gain,
It means he did not die in vain,
He put me here to face a trial,
I hope he thinks it all worthwhile.

I know that if I play my part,
God is always in my heart,
That's why I'll never be alone,
Even though it seems I'm on my own.

DREAMS OF HOME

I've always been a working man,
For work I had to roam,
Yet I always dreamed of Ireland,
The place I knew as home.

I'd dream that I was on a ship,
As it reached Ireland's green shore,
Though I'd been away for many a year,
I still loved her more and more.

I would feel my eyes go misty,
As around the Bay I'd cast,
To see that old Black Mountain,
As it stood o'er dear Belfast.

I'd think of her green countryside,
'Twas there in my minds eye,
How her mountains and her trees,
Both reached up to the sky.

I would picture my dear village,
I was with my friends again,
I could see that floor of Bluebells,
In Lord Caledon's vast Demesne.

Once again I saw her countryside,
With whins and gorse galore,
Still I'd picture Enagh Lough,
With me there on her shore.

I'd see again the Blackwater,
A picture that makes me sigh,
How I'd love to be upon her banks,
As her waters passed me by.

I'd picture walks on the old Red Brae,
I still see it in my dream,
As it swept down to a hollow,
Where it crossed a tiny stream.

I'd love to see my dear Tyrone,
I'd go there if I could,
To take a walk through Brantry,
To see once more her wood.

I'd see again dear old Creeve Lough,
Oh' how that I do wish,
To see once more that Brantry shore,
'Twas there we used to fish.

My mind springs back to the present,
I drop to my knees and pray,
That I will catch that steamer,
And see Ireland soon someday.

For when it comes my turn to die,
I want it to be seen,
That I was buried in Ireland,
Beneath those sods of green.

Still I'll look back on my life,
To think how it was grand,
To have lived my life so happily,
Though not in my native land.

I hope I go to Heaven,
For then I'll feel at home,
With all that beauty around me,
Sure I'll think it's still Tyrone.

A REMINDER TO THE HUMAN RACE

Have you ever watched a glowing Sunrise,
As it peeps o'er the morning mist,
To see this vapour of beauty,
Is a picture that Nature has kissed.

Have you ever heard the morning choir,
As it soars to reach each note,
If we possessed this Godly gift,
I'm sure we would strut and gloat.

Have you noticed as the day progresses,
Natures beauty it seems to vanish,
It must have something to do with us,
Natural beauty it seems we must banish.

The choirs song is drowned by noise,
Natures beauty we take it for granted,
We never notice the array of wild flowers,
Or the trees that Nature has planted.

We scurry around for most of the day,
'Tis a time we lose our sight,
Nature gains control once more,
With the coming of the peaceful night.

It's then we notice the Sun once more,
At the time when it must set,
It paints the sky with golden splendour,
How lucky can we humans get.

It's then that quietness descends once more,
And the birds do sweetly sing,
If only the daytime could be like this,
It would be such a wonderful thing.

Why destroy Mother Nature's work,
Why always try to spoil,
The lavishness of her beauty,
Or the earthiness of her soil.

We continue to pollute the waterways,
We destroy the freshness in the air,
Why do we do these horrid things,
It seems we just don't care.

Mother Nature is always generous,
Yet our actions have been a disgrace,
why not accept the things she's given,
To put a smile back on her face.

Must we destroy this Planet Earth,
A solution must surely be found,
Before we blot out those Heavenly skies,
Or destroy this life giving ground.

We were given the things of life,
Fertile soil to supply us our food,
Water was meant to give us life,
Why is it that we must intrude.

Why don't we try to clasp her hand,
Don't try to compete or compare,
Keep the earth and the water pure,
And keep the freshness in our air.

If we don't try to help Mother Nature,
Our future it hasn't a prayer,
We'll have thrown away her greatest gift,
To fall victim to the Ozone Layer.

MY NANCY

Many years ago I met a girl,
And she said her name was Nancy,
Ah' boys she was so lovely,
So to her I took a fancy.

I plucked up all my courage,
And I asked her for a date,
She said yes... and called me dear,
So I felt it must be fate.

Our first date was a Summer's walk,
As the birds did bill and coo,
I slipped my arm around her waist,
Well... you know the way you do.

She was a very tall girl,
With long blond flowing locks,
And me being a small chap,
Had to stand on an apple box.

I took a chance to steal a kiss,
From her lovely rounded lip,
But before I made a contact,
'Twas then I chose to slip.

So I tumbled from my apple box,
And fell on to the grass,
My dear Nancy sat beside me,
That lovely fair haired lass.

Says she I have to tell you this,
If not 'twould be unfair,
What you see is a blond wig,
For I have got no hair.

Perhaps I have misled you,
Forgive me please I beg,
For what you see me standing on,
Is a solid wooden leg.

When first I did entice you,
I winked when you did pass,
That eye I have to tell you,
Is made from marble glass.

When you did whisper those sweet words,
With no attention being paid,
You see my dear... I couldn't hear,
For I'd lost my hearing aid.

I'd better tell you everything,
Then you will know the truth,
Everything I have is false,
Sure I haven't got a tooth.

I took a look at my dear Nancy,
At first I felt despair,
And yet the more I looked at her,
The less I seemed to care.

I thought about the price of perms,
And the Dentist can be dear,
She wouldn't be fit to hear... or chase me,
And yon eye would shed no tear.

So I took a hold of my dear Nancy,
And her face lit up with glee,
For she knew that what was left of her,
Was good enough for me.

THOUGHTS OF CHILDHOOD

Oh' to sit on a river's bank,
To watch languid waters flow by,
To think and dwell of times long gone,
And the memories that make me sigh.

'Twas here I spent my childhood days,
Which I see in the hazy past,
Those days they seemed so happy,
And we thought they'd always last.

Yet childhood days soon pass us by,
When we played with never a care,
We scuffed our shoes and got dirty,
And our clothes we'd always tear.

'Twas a time of many friendships,
How we thought they'd always last,
Yet to-day... I don't hear their laughter,
Only echoes that ring from the past.

I think of all my friends at school,
In their midst I felt secure,
I thought they'd be there always,
Now to-day... I'm not so sure.

I remember our minds were innocent,
How we played and acted the fool,
How we felt so happy and carefree,
As we made our way home from school.

We'd think of lots of things to do,
To make mischief and games to play,
We'd likely forget our homework,
And the things our teacher did say.

We oft did play at marbles,
Maybe tig or hide and seek,
We might fish, hunt... or roam the fields,
Many things could be done in a week.

We had our own way of showing affection,
As nicknames abounded galore,
Like Jaunty, Gunner, Polar and Kate,
And I know there were many more.

We often played our games bare footed,
Yet our feet were no less fleet,
Still I hear those shouts of joy,
As we ran on the cobbled street.

Girls and boys played make believe,
'Twas a time we could all pretend,
We never had a reason to think,
That our childhood days would end.

There seemed to be nothing but happiness,
We never knew of a word called grief,
The only sadness of our childhood,
Was its time was all too brief.

Our parents they tried to tell us,
How this was the best time in life,
How later on as adults,
We'd meet with some trouble and strife.

Still I hear the echo of their words,
I can't help but give a sigh,
Like the waters of the flowing river,
My childhood has passed me by.

LET'S

Wouldn't it be an awful thing,
That if our life should end,
With no one we had loved,
Or one to call a friend.

How silly to wish our time away,
It passes with such haste,
And if-not used as it should be,
Then our time has been a waste.

Let's try to brighten every day,
On your face please wear a grin,
Let's try to keep out gloom,
Just let the Sun shine in.

Let's create an atmosphere,
That's full of joy and fun,
Let's try to lend a helping hand,
And be good to everyone.

Let's help to feed the hungry,
In those countries far away,
They too deserve to have,
Some sunshine in their day.

Let's help the sick both near and far,
All those who need our aid,
Let's do it from our heart,
Never think of being paid.

Let's not scorn at those who help,
And work for charities galore,
Let's think of how you too can help,
Remember... there's room for more.

Let's give thanks to the God above,
For the gift of oft good health,
Let's give a thought to the poor,
Who have not gained your wealth.

Let's think of the Gates of Heaven,
Will they open to let you through,
Let's think of what you'll say,
When asked... what did you do.

Did you feed the hungry,
When asked... did you say no,
Did you refuse to aid the sick,
Or the poor in times of woe.

Let's think about these questions,
And the answers you will give,
For God will give his judgement,
On the way you chose to live.

If all your answers are no,
Please take heed of this rhyme,
Change your answers to yes,
While God still gives you time.

A MOTHER

A mother is the person,
Who tucked us up in bed,
She taught to us our prayers,
And words that must be said.

She helped you to your feet,
And taught you how to talk,
She helped you with your first step,
As you did learn to walk.

She was always at your side,
When you did give a call,
She was always there to pick you up,
At times when you did fall.

Her face was full of tenderness,
Her love was plain to see,
As she tried to ease the pain,
From that cut upon your knee.

As she nursed you through sickness,
Many times she breathed a sigh,
As she wiped away the tear,
That had fallen from your eye.

She helped to ease your pain,
She helped you cut that tooth,
She helped you through your schooldays,
She prepared you for your youth.

She had only one ambition for you,
And that was to make you live,
For that, she'd give her own dear life,
And all that she could give.

She always gave the best she had,
No reward... did she ever seek,
Just the hug you wished to give,
Or that kiss upon her cheek.

You'll remember how she listened,
To all your tales of woe,
And how her heart did break,
When you said... you'd have to go.

How when you went to work,
And the world you had to roam,
While your mother was alive,
You always had a home.

Though you couldn't always see her,
You knew she played her part,
She was never far from you,
You were always in her heart.

We'll think of all those early days,
When we were girls and boys,
How she did feed and clothe us,
And gave us sweets and toys.

Let's hope that we will do her proud,
And do what e'er we should,
Let us hope... that we all did,
The best for her we could.

For even if she's dead and gone,
And lives in that Heaven above,
She'll always try to guide you,
And to fill your life with love.

NO RETURN

When e'er it comes my turn to die,
I will ne'er want back again,
For I couldn't stand the aggro,
Nor I couldn't stand the pain.

I couldn't bear the evil,
Nor help to plant its seed,
I couldn't stand the jealousy,
Nor I couldn't stand the greed.

Oh' how I'd hate to face a life,
Where falsehood was the theme,
With a world so full of cheating,
Doing good was just a dream.

How you had to be so cunning,
Just to make oneself seem smart,
How it was great to tell a lie,
And to swear was such an art.

It didn't matter who you hurt,
You said the words you feel,
And if you couldn't afford a thing,
It was proper then to steal.

There was always a need to fight,
It didn't matter what for,
Man would fight his fellow man,
They loved to go to war.

So when I think of all these things,
No longer do I dread,
That I have gone forever,
To join the countless dead.

THOUGHTS

Oh' how hard this life can be,
And the toll that it can take,
How it's so unforgiving,
If we make a small mistake.

Yet life can be so kind,
It depends on how we live,
Do we always want to take,
And never want to give.

Do we always want to criticise,
And never give a praise,
Do we always try to darken,
Instead of brighten days.

Do we always break our word,
And play life's silly pranks,
Do we ever show concern,
Do we ever offer thanks.

Does your mind have evil thoughts,
Have you a heart of stone,
Do you ever do a good deed,
And for misdeeds to atone.

If you should show a kindness,
And try always to forgive,
Then life can be so beautiful,
And a pleasure for to live.

THE CALEDON OF OLD
(*1920 Period*)

I wish to tell a story,
Of a village I know well,
It's the one we know as Caledon,
The place where I do dwell.

I've listened to the old folks,
And the stories they did tell,
About times in the twenties,
When the Mill was working well.

They told me of those long gone days,
And the people they'd likely meet,
How times they were so peaceful,
With no cars there on the street.

Mr. Graham was a prominent man,
It's so easy for to tell,
For he owned a shop and 'The Caledon Inn'
And 'The Caledon Arms' as well.

Scott Bros had their grocery and coal,
At the foot of the old Church-Hill,
They were one of many grocers,
'Twas thanks to the old Woollen Mill.

For we had McVeigh's and Miss Donnelly,
We had Mercer's and Robinson's too,
There was Duncan's and 'Old Ma Farl's'
They were grocers fine and true.

There was Mrs, Ferguson and Miss Wilton,
They saw to the Drapery trade,
And Mr. Ferguson was a Saddler,
The best that could be made.

Mr. Knox and Mr. Morrow were the Butchers,
They made it so hard to choose,
Miss Wigglesworth ran a homely shop,
Where all could buy their shoes.

There was Harry McMullan and Mr. Forde,
They both had a Tailor's trade,
And Miss Stewart was a Dressmaker,
What frocks that lady made.

We had Frank Campbell and Mrs Stringer,
Who sold Ice Cream, sweets and more,
There was two sisters... the Miss Johnston's
Who traded fancy goods galore.

Tommy Drennan would fix our bicycles,
Johnny Watson was a Blacksmith by trade,
Doctor Patterson was a skilled G.P.
Who oft came to our aid.

Mr. Graham ran 'The Caledon Inn'
And Mrs. McKenna 'The Corner Bar'
Mr. Woods too owned a public house,
For those who liked a jar.

Mr. Williams he had a 'Post Office'
'Twas at the Armagh end of town,
And like all these other people,
Was a person of great renown.

Oh' to think of these people,
Who lived in those early years,
They worked so hard to help us,
They knew little of the fears.

They little thought how shops would close,
Though much against their will,
There was little else for them to do,
When they closed that old 'Woollen Mill,

How later on in years to come,
No longer would they greet,
The old 'Clogher Valley' Railway,
As it chugged along their street.

All these people have long since gone,
They've trod their path in life,
They saw our village in happy times,
And they saw its time of strife.

All of them... they did their best,
'Twas not they who chose,
To kill their greatest asset,
When 'The Mill' it had to close.

Life travels on much faster now,
Long gone is that gentle pace,
When people had time to look around,
And care for the human race.

We don't support our local shop,
We'd rather use our car,
And go to shop in other towns,
In towns both near and far.

We should think of those bygone days,
That linger in the hazy past,
And think of all the peaceful times,
And why... they couldn't last.

For in those days of contentment,
There was many a pitfall in life,
But there was always a helping hand,
When there came that time of strife.

In those days there seemed no hurry,
And people had time to see,
If there was need for a helping hand.
To people like you and me.

So listen to what the old folks say,
And the stories that were told,
Then maybe we too... can be content,
Like those in the days of old.

HEAVEN'S GATE

An old woman stood at Heaven's gate,
Her face wrinkled by the years,
And though she'd always, done her best,
Her heart was filled with fears.

Yet once she saw Saint Peter's face,
How it bore a friendly grin,
She felt there was a good chance,
That he would let her in.

She hoped to see her eldest son,
To see his face once more,
She remembered how he looked,
As he marched off to war.

He fought with all his might,
He felt right was on his side,
Otherwise he'd never have gone,
To that place where he had died.

She thought about the sad years,
That she had spent on Earth,
She thought about her youngest child,
How it had died at birth.

She knew she'd see her parents,
For they were good and kind,
'Twas they who taught her right from wrong,
And of the peace she'd find.

She thought about her many friends,
How she'd mourned them in the past,
Now she knew the time had come,
When those friendships were to last.

As she stood and looked at Peter,
His hand did brush her face,
'Twas then he opened the gate
And gave to her a place.

She glanced inside with wonderment,
Many thoughts did crowd her mind,
She thought of all the people,
Still to follow on behind.

If only they could see this place,
Free from trouble and strife,
They'd make Earth more like Heaven,
They'd change their way of life.

They would do away with war and greed,
And not rule with an iron rod,
The rich would deal with poverty,
And the proud would kneel to God.

Yet she knew it could never happen,
For their sins they must atone,
Before they share God's goodness,
Or kneel before his throne.

THANKING GOD

Sometimes this world looks gloomy,
Yet it's not that way with me,
For I thank God for the people,
That he placed on earth with me.

Some supply me with entertainment,
With music, laughter and song,
God has done his best for us,
It's we who've done it wrong.

I thank him for the inventors,
Who give me the comforts in life,
Also the tradesmen and medics,
Who hold at bay my strife.

I thank him for the colours,
And the beauty that he sends,
I thank him for the skies above,
And I thank him for my friends.

I thank him for this lovely Earth,
It's so beautiful and round,
I thank him for the waters,
And I thank him for the ground.

I thank him for the animals,
And the life that's in our seas,
I thank him for the plant life,
The flowers, grass and trees.

I thank him for the Moon and Stars,
And the gift of a dazzling Sun,
I thank him for the Seasons,
And the way he makes them run.

I thank him for the Bird life,
And the songs that they do sing,
They herald each coming dawn,
And tell of the budding Spring.

I thank him for my birth,
That enabled me to see,
All these wondrous things,
That he placed on Earth for me.

Yet all these things are useless,
If our outlook isn't bright,
God didn't make this Planet,
To put us in a plight.

So let's enjoy the gifts he gave,
And the love he always sends,
Let's spread the word he gave us,
And make all Nations friends.

To all the people in this world,
I want for you to see,
I'm glad you're here upon this Earth,
At the very same time as me.

NOT SO BLIND

One day I met a stranger,
I knew that he was blind,
My heart was full of pity,
As I thought to be so kind.

I thought perhaps I'd help him,
And perform a noble deed,
Gently... he declined my hand,
He said there was no need.

'Twas then he put me at my ease,
He said to have no fear,
For I can see a picture,
Just as long as I can hear.

If I can hear that rippling sound,
I couldn't ask for more,
For I can see those gentle waves,
As they lap upon the shore.

Sometimes I hear a swirling wind,
Or just a gentle breeze,
If I can hear a rustling sound,
Then I can see the trees.

Sometimes I listen to the notes,
As a feathered friend does sing,
And if I hear a fluttering,
I see birds upon the wing.

Sometimes I listen to silence,
When there seems to be no sound,
'Tis then I see the snowflakes,
As they flutter to the ground.

'Tis oft I've heard the happiness,
In a mother's gentle sigh,
'Tis then I see a new born child,
As I hear it give a cry.

Sometimes I hear the insect life,
As it flits upon the wing,
Sometimes I see a tree branch sway
As I hear it creak and swing.

For me there are so many sounds,
Yet my picture's not always clear,
For me... it's a simple matter,
I try harder for to hear.

For when I listen to those sounds,
A picture comes to mind,
For it's only when you're deaf,
That you are really blind.

So go my friend and be happy,
And please don't pity me,
The only person who is really blind,
Is the one who will not see.

THE OLD RED BRAE

I love to walk on the old Red Brae,
It's here my thoughts they drool,
I recall the times I've passed this way,
With the friends I knew at school.

Sunshine filled those far off days,
'Twas happiness that filled our dish,
As we laughed, joked and made merry,
God granted our every wish.

I think mostly of the Summer time,
That wondrous time of year,
As we trod our path on the old Red Brae,
The future ... it held no fear.

Yet now as the years have rolled by,
And I walk here all alone,
A tear is close to my eye,
For my friends have all left their home.

Still I hear their echo of laughter,
At the silly little things they would say,
Still I feel their presence around me,
As I walk on the old Red Brae.

In my mind there lurks a question,
And I know what it's trying to say,
"Do all those friends of yesteryear,
Still think of the old Red Brae"

Yet I feel my friends can never forget,
They will never be left behind,
Still they'll walk on the old Red Brae,
While trapped here in my mind.

It matters not that they've left me,
Or how far that they had to roam,
For when I walk on the old Red Brae,
They are always close to their home.

I oft do wonder if they think of me,
Be it any night or day,
Do they see me with a smiling face,
On the slopes of the old Red Brae.

Do they know how much I do miss them,
How I loved them so very much,
How at times they seem so close to me,
I feel I could reach out and touch.

Never will I let them leave my mind,
I doubt if they'd want to try,
For through me... they'll walk this path,
Till it comes my turn to die.

Yet somehow I know that they're happy,
I feel I know what they'd say,
"How happy we are to be in your mind,
As you walk on the old Red Brae"

God has been so good to me,
I'm pleased with what he's done,
To let me think of all my friends,
And to make us feel as one.

For that's the way it feels to me,
Whose friends who I still love to-day,
Are here in my mind and my body,
As I walk on the old Red Brae.

I feel I'm part of God's master plan,
He never meant for me to roam,
I was meant to walk on the old Red Brae,
So my friends would be closer to home.

If that was his plan... then I'm happy,
I'm glad that he did what he did,
I'm happier still on the old Red Brae,
When I know what I do is his bid.

When the time comes... as it surely must do,
And I walk for the very last time,
On those lovely slopes of the old Red Brae,
And to put an end to this rhyme.

I'll hand the reins to someone else,
And to them I'll have this to say,
"Please give a thought to the people,
Who have walked on the old Red Brae"

FEATHERED FRIENDS

I've heard the call of the Cuckoo,
To herald a brand new Spring,
I've heard the Thrush and Finch,
And the songs they love to sing.

The Sparrow and the Robin,
How they chirp the whole day long,
And the Lark brings in the night,
With its own sweet lilting song.

I've listened to the chirping Wren,
And the Blue Tit at its best,
I've heard the cawing of Rooks,
As they make their way to nest.

I've listened to the Curlew,
As it made its plaintive cry,
The Blackbird shrills its warning,
As a danger passes by.

I've listened to the Wood-Pigeon,
As it made its loving coo,
Especially at the breaking dawn,
When the grass was spread with dew.

I've watched the Swift and Swallow,
As they dive to make their sweep,
I've listened to the Corn-Crake,
As I've tried to go to sleep.

How lucky we are to have our birds,
And the music they do rend,
Our world would be so empty,
Without our feathered friend.

CHRISTMAS THOUGHTS

The nicest thing there is for me,
Is to see the glow of a Christmas tree,
Covered with tinsel and sprayed with frost,
To me its beauty is never lost.

Those hanging bells, the stout balloon,
Herald the coming of Santa soon,
Twinkling lights they shine nonstop,
The little fairy stands on top.

Still I have that child's belief,
For I see presents lie underneath,
When people ask... I tend to pause,
How can they doubt there's a Santa Claus.

On Christmas morn I'm full of glee,
Has Santa left a gift for me,
I creep downstairs... I feel so queer,
I hope' I pray' that Santa's here.

I feast my eyes on what I see,
Presents lie 'neath the Christmas Tree,
Santa's been... I shed a tear,
How silly I was to have a fear.

Yet Christmas is not for presents galore,
It's the birth of Christ, who gave us more,
He gave his life that we might live,
The greatest gift that he could give.

As we reach the end of Christmas day,
I hope we didn't forget to pray,
To thank God for his only son,
That's the gift with no paper on.

For it's a gift so hard to see,
It may not be at the Christmas Tree,
And yet that gift it was so dear,
A gift that lasts for every year.

Yet God allows our mind to stray,
He too enjoys his Christmas Day,
He'll share his day... simply because,
Your love and joy, are his Santa Claus.

SANTA

Christmas time is coming,
And the snow is building high,
Santa Claus is coming,
With his reindeers in the sky.

What presents will he bring us,
Piled up on his sleigh,
We must go to bed and sleep,
And wait for Christmas Day.

For Santa Claus is coming,
In that I do believe,
We'll see him soon, across the moon,
Upon a Christmas Eve.

A TREE'S VIEWPOINT

When e'er I look at once green trees,
Now that Autumn has touched our leaves,
I can see our glow is jaded,
Our verdure green is crimped and faded.

For us of course there's no relief,
Autumn will take each single leaf,
And all my friends so great and tall,
Can only watch as their leaves fall.

We watch our clothing fall to ground,
It seems to fall with ne'er a sound,
Yet life returns when birds do sing,
New buds appear with early Spring.

We watch our buds unfurl in wild,
To us they are a new born child,
Soon we see our splendour grow,
Yet come the Autumn, 'twill have to go.

Do you ever give a thought to me,
Even though I'm just a tree,
All I ask is please be fair,
You breath the good we give to air.

Why should we have to suffer strife,
As vandals hack and spoil our life,
If only you could see my frown,
You'd never want to cut me down.

Sometimes I look and see a space,
Where friends of mine they once did grace,
For those lost friends I shed a tear,
I seem to shed them every year.

Yet all my friends did offer shade,
To those who lay in yonder glade,
So please I hope you'll heed my plea,
Don't cut me down... just let me be.

FUTILITY

A young soldier went to war,
Though much against his will,
He didn't want to fight,
Nor he didn't want to kill.

A young soldier went to war,
He turned to wave goodbye,
He felt it was the last time,
For we heard him give a sigh.

A young soldier went to war,
They gave to him a gun,
They said he had to fight,
Until the war was won.

A young soldier went to war,
He never asked them why,
He didn't want to fight,
Nor he didn't want to die.

A young soldier went to war,
To face the battle's strife,
Why did he have to fight,
Why did he give his life.

A HOPE

I hope to go to Heaven,
That place so good and grand,
I hope for God's sweet goodness,
As he takes me by the hand.

I hope he will accept me,
His Kingdom for to serve,
I'll hope that he is lenient,
For his love I don't deserve.

He'll know I wasn't perfect,
And was prone to make mistake,
Yet I hope he knows I love him,
And knows I'm not a fake.

'Twas he who placed me on this earth,
He set for me a test,
I hope he gives a pass mark,
For I did my human best.

Sometimes my best... it wasn't good,
'Tis now that I could cry,
If tears could wash my Soul,
I would have no fear to die.

I hope that God is merciful,
To give benefit of the doubt,
To give to me a second chance,
And will not cast me out.

It's so easy to feel sorry,
As we stand before God's glance,
Our world would be so different,
If we had that other chance.

I hope that man will think of this,
With the time he spends on earth,
For life begins at death,
And death begins at birth.

GREATNESS

I know a woman of greatness,
Her faith is never thin,
She'll never judge a person,
By the colour of their skin.

She spends her life just giving,
She does what good she can,
She's always very gentle,
Be it woman, child or man.

This Planet should be grateful,
That her presence it did grace,
This earth with love and modesty,
For to make a better place.

Her hands are blessed with healing,
She gives what she can give,
For her there's one ambition,
In that others... they might live.

God did place her on this earth,
To lead this worthy life,
I'm proud to know this woman,
I'm proud to call her wife.

DIANA
(The People's Princess)

You lived, you loved, you cared,
All these gifts with us you shared,
You were never distant, you were never vain,
You sought to see that we would gain.

You didn't confine your work to home,
You helped the world where'er you'd roam,
Where there was hunger, you would appear,
Where there was pain, you'd dry a tear.

You fought a cause each living day,
You trod a path where landmines lay,
You spoke to those whose heart was hard,
But you were always a winning card.

A winning card for many parts,
A winning card, the Queen of hearts,
Heads of state who spoke to you,
Knew their duty and what to do.

You did your duties with care and grace,
You made our world a better place,
Yet still we feel our life so poor,
We wished you'd lived a few years more.

For in our life you played your part,
Many times you lightened a heavy heart,
How often you eased the pain of fear,
As you hugged a child stained by a tear.

Now you have gone, our life is grim,
You're at God's side, to stand by him,
But your efforts were not in vain,
We'll tell you all, when we meet again.

OLD COINS

Old coins they are so wonderful,
They stand the years so well,
Oh' the sights they've seen,
What stories they could tell.

When e'er I look at these old coins,
My heart does heave a sigh,
I think of all the Kings and Queens,
Who lived in years gone-by.

I think too of their subjects,
Who did handle this old coin,
They had to work so very hard,
To make ends meet and join.

Some Monarchs reigned for many years,
They served to rule their state,
Other reigns were very short,
When forced to abdicate.

Some Rulers died before their time,
As troops they would rebel,
What difference this to history,
It's very hard to tell.

What trials and tribulations,
These old coins have seen,
They've seen the hand of poverty,
And the hand of King and Queen.

Rich or poor, they've passed away,
They helped plant history's seed,
Some held these coins for food to live,
Some held these coins for greed.

THE OLD STONE BRIDGE

As I gaze around my village grand,
There are many sights to see,
But there's a certain roadway,
That means so much to me.

As I walk along the Armagh road,
I oft do pause a while,
To gaze upon the crooked steps,
Of that dear old fashioned stile.

This stile leads to an Old Stone Bridge,
Where the 'Mill Race' once did pass,
'Twas there I used to watch it flow,
Now all I see is grass.

That bridge did serve for many years,
As "The Race' flowed from a sluice,
It makes me sigh to see it dry,
And no longer put to use.

How oft a crowd did cross that bridge,
For a football match to see,
Still I hear the tread of feet,
Yet to-day there's only me.

In my dream, I see a football team,
As they play between yon posts,
'Tis only they who use this pitch,
As they flit about like ghosts.

Yet as I gaze o'er that old bridge wall,
Once more I start to dream,
In rushing waters I see a Trout,
As it tries to swim upstream.

Before I leave that dear old bridge,
Once more I pause a while,
I think of those who've passed this way,
As they stepped down from the stile.

I think I see their ghosts go by,
As their chatter fills the air,
Of me… they take no notice,
As they pass without life's care.

Oh' to think of those joyous days,
What a pity they had to pass,
And pity too that Old Stone Bridge,
With nothing to see but grass,

Yet still that bridge it has a use,
For when it greets my eye,
It makes me think of the happy days,
When 'The Mill Race' passed it by.

LIFE'S DREAM

It's funny how we always seem,
To be so happy in a dream,
Yet when it's time for us to wake,
We think our dream's a big mistake.

It's funny how in proper life,
We seem so bent on war and strife,
If only we would try to live,
To be forgiving and to give.

Then to us our life would seem,
To be the same as in our dream,
And in the morn when we awake,
We'd never make the same mistake.

LAST THOUGHTS

As I lie here weak from illness,
I feel no thought of dread,
Inside my heart, I feel relief,
Though soon I may be dead.

For I see a world in turmoil,
I see nothing here but strife,
So please... I want no mourning,
With the passing of my life.

I wish to thank my loved ones,
Who did their best for me,
For them... I'd like to stay,
But its not meant to be.

I'll always think of my birthplace,
I'll never forget its name,
Even though it too has changed,
And can never be the same.

All the old folks they have gone,
They were full of love and Care,
People to-day... have a different way,
This change I couldn't bear.

Most people have no time to speak,
And their thoughts they mount to nil,
Soon I'll be in a better place,
A place so quiet and still.

So when I go... as I surely will,
It's hard to know just when,
I'll thank God for my life span,
For I've passed three score and ten.

SUBTLETY

Death is a very final thing,
We heard a good man sigh,
I hope I never take a life,
Not to even squash a fly.

So this other noble man,
Paid heed to what was said,
He never squashed a fly,
He sprayed the fly instead.

As the fly it lay a fluttering,
It spoke up to the man,
"That stuff was very bitter,
What had you in that can"

The man bent down and answered,
"It's a spray for flies of course"
Said the fly "I wish you'd squashed me,
For I think that stuff is worse"

Yer man took pity on the little fly,
As it lay in a dying state,
Says he "Please try to stay alive,
It may not be too late"

So yer man went and got a stick,
Says he "I'll do my bit"
That little fly... didn't die from spray,
For yer man he went and squashed it.

MORNING BLISS

I love to walk in early morn,
'Tis the best time I have spent,
To see the sights before me,
They were surely Heaven sent.

'Tis then I pause as if in trance,
As the daylight peeks around,
My heart's content and full at ease,
With my breath the only sound.

To stand upon a crest of hill,
To drink that morning view,
Like the rising mist before me,
Or the flora drenched with dew.

To see the Sun rise o'er the land,
To herald a brand new day,
To hear the birds in tuneful song,
As the rabbits hop in play.

To hear the yelp of a weary fox,
Tired from its nightly roam,
For it... the Dawn's a warning,
As it treads a path for home.

The morning air does pinch my cheek,
Oh' how I love it so,
I can almost touch the silence,
And the grass I hear it grow.

I feel at peace with all the world,
I'm thrilled I did not miss,
All this beauty that Nature gives,
And the glory of a mornings bliss.

Soon I too must tread for home,
This beauty will soon be gone,
Yet still my heart does quicken,
As I think of the morrow's morn.

WISHFUL THINKING

It was a bright and lovely morn,
As I dressed up in my best,
I splashed my face with aftershave,
Then put it to the test.

I thought it best to mingle,
But soon 'twas plain to see,
The aftershave... it didn't work,
For no-one noticed me.

It was then I saw the Queen,
As her carriage it drove by,
And I swear she looked at me,
Then winked with her right eye.

The aftershave was working,
What else was I to think,
Until the Queen was heard to say,
"One's eye is on the blink"

'Twas then I did awaken,
'Twas not as it did seem,
For I hadn't even shaved,
The whole thing was a dream.

THE LONG WEEK
(After Princess Diana Died)

Oh' how my heart was hurt and torn,
As I watched a nation weep and mourn,
I watched a flower mountain grow,
A Nation's sorrow... it had to show.

Millions came to say good-bye,
Most did sob and give a cry,
Some... didn't know what to say,
Most... hardly knew the time of day.

The Nation it seemed, just wanted to share,
To show Diana that they did care,
And always there came the question... why,
'Twas then a tear would come to eye.

Why did that car speed with such haste,
Why did that crash cause such a waste,
Why is it... that God he chose
To pluck from us our brightest Rose.

Oh' that week it seemed so long,
From that fateful morn, till Elton's song,
As we watched Diana go to her rest,
Millions of emotions were put to test.

To learn from her... I'll have to try,
To be so brave and not to cry,
I just hope... I'll pass the test,
For tears they well up in my chest.

For our Diana... she showed no fear,
No-one saw her shed a tear,
'She showed the Nation her brightest face,
She walked so tall and with such grace.

But now it's time to say good-bye,
To follow you... we'll have to try,
Good-bye Diana... we all loved you,
We'll try to make your dreams come true.

SORROW IS PEACE

When asked... if I felt sorry,
I said I did of course,
For I pitied any man who lived,
Who's never felt remorse.

One only has to think of God,
Who just before he died,
Forgave the thief with sorrow,
Who was hanging at his side.

It's right to feel such sorrow,
It's a reason why we live,
And the reason that we feel it,
Is to make us all forgive.

To forgive... it is a virtue,
A virtue that God allowed,
So when you hear of sorrow,
To forgive... will make you proud.

When asked if you've felt sorry,
Answer yes with all your pride,
For without it... you can't forgive,
And peace would leave your side.

THE MASTER GARDENER

I love to rest in my garden of dreams,
Where my heart has never a care,
It's my nearest place to Heaven,
For I feel that God is there.

When I see that host of colours,
Which make for a wondrous scene,
Each touched by the Master's hand,
With the lawns of verdure green.

I work to keep my garden's splendour,
I'll nurture the plant to grow,
But I am just the tool of God,
It's he who created this show.

Who is it that makes the Sun shine,
And spreads the morning dew,
Who put the scent in the roses,
Who painted the Bluebells blue.

Just think of all the species,
And the beauty that they gain,
Only God could deem to make them,
All we do... is supply a name.

Who else could have thought of a snowdrop,
With a purity like that of a child,
Or the Daisy... the Buttercup... or Cowslip,
Those flowers that grow in the wild.

The wild flowers tell the true story,
They grow the whole year round,
They don't seem to need a gardener,
To nurture their growth in the ground.

Sometimes we try to destroy them,
God's face... it must wear a frown,
As we try to undo his masterplan,
By spraying or mowing them down.

Yet still they blossom every year,
How is it... that they survive,
They had no gardener to guide them,
Who is it that keeps them alive.

Now back to those garden flowers,
That were nurtured and given a guide,
'Tis plain they do not need it,
Just think of their friends in the wild.

My garden, it gives me much pleasure,
My duty... I never would shirk,
To help with God's creation,
To help with the menial work.

As I try to picture Heaven,
And the way I'd like it best,
I just look around my garden,
As I sit to take my rest.

For a garden is like a Kingdom,
Its sight is a beautiful thing,
The nicest thing... God did for me,
Was to place me as its King.

When next you admire a garden,
Don't praise any woman or man,
For they are just the tools of God,
They too... are part of his plan.

MY WIFE IS MY LIFE

As I reach the end of another year,
My thoughts they start to play,
I think of what my wife has done,
It's more than words can say.

I'm so lucky to be her husband,
She sees when I am down,
A soothing touch from her gentle hand,
Soon wipes away my frown.

It's hard to recall... all that she's done,
So of some I'll take my pick,
I think of days when I felt fed up,
How she helped me... when I was sick.

In days when I had self doubt,
I would feel I couldn't cope,
She was always there beside me,
To fill my life with hope.

If I could compare her to a Temple,
Her heart would be the dome,
Her body... would be its altar,
And her mind would make it a home.

For she is the brightness in my life,
She's as gentle as a Turtle Dove,
The greatest gift she has for me,
Is the depth of her great love.

I do my best to return her love,
Yet I know that I am beat,
When I think of all her goodness,
I know I can't compete.

Her love for me shines from her eye,,
She fills my life with laughter,
She has the gift of healing hands,
To compete... I'd be a non starter.

Yet there again... why should I compete,
After all... I'm only a man,
I'll do my best to make her happy,
I'll do the best that I can.

In love I'm rich... I'm happy to say,
Her goodness is plain to see,
I also know... why our marriage is strong,
She works twice as hard as me.

This year like all the others,
Is the happiest that there has been,
If future years compare with the past,
It's thanks to my dear Colleen.

In the years to come... I hope she's happy,
I will do the best that I can,
And yet you see... it may not be enough,
After all... I'm only a man.

AN ARMCHAIR VIEW

One night as I sat at my fire,
I stared at the glowing embers,
I could see my whole community,
And those who were its members.

I could see again the May Blossom,
As it swayed on branches strong,
I could see again my parents,
They taught me right from wrong.

Once more I stood on the Armagh road,
There was a Monument... so great and tall,
I'm pained to see an explosion,
'Twas that which made it fall.

I could see once more the soldiers huts,
'Twas here the soldiers stayed,
Yet to us... it was a Venue,
Where a marbles game was played.

Still I see a haunched figure,
How he chased us again and again,
It's Peter Taylor... the Gamekeeper,
Who guarded Lord Caledon's Demesne.

There then appears Kilgowney Wood,
It's here we used to play,
Sometimes... we'd pick wild strawberries,
Just to pass the time of day.

I wish I could see many other things,
But I... must leave you in doubt,
Don't blame me... it's not my fault,
The fire you see... has gone out.

THE CLOGHER VALLEY TRAIN

When I think of my dear village,
In the days when all was fine,
When that Clogher Valley Train,
Came chugging down its line.

As it made its way from Tynan,
For that's where it came from,
My heart would start to beat,
Like that beating on a drum.

As it steamed in to our village,
It would pass our thriving Mill,
Then chug right down our Main Street,
Sure I think I see it still.

That train it served the Valley well,
How well... it's hard to gauge,
That dear old fashioned steamer,
That served a different age.

No more do I hear that sound,
Which I loved when as a boy,
As she gave a whistle blast,
On her way to Aughnacloy.

That train is part of history now,
No more that train we'll greet,
For now there's not a sign,
Of its tracks there on our Street.

Yet if I listen hard enough,
A sound in my mind does grow,
I can hear that train a puffing,
And I hear that whistle blow.

THE CHANCE

There was a man in my townland,
I can't recall his name,
Most people thought him sinful,
And he always took the blame.

Some would ask me what I thought,
Why was this man so bad,
I found I could not answer,
For my heart was dull and sad.

I thought about what God did say,
The best words that I've known,
"Let him who has not sinned,
Be the first to cast a stone"

I thought about these words,
What a state my mind was in,
What answer could I give,
For I wasn't free from sin.

I looked at those who asked me,
I could see they wanted blood,
I couldn't throw that first stone,
But I wondered... if they could.

I told them of my thoughts,
And to leave this man alone,
Their hearts were full of guilt,
As each hand... did hold a stone.

Yet not a stone was cast at him,
As they thought of what I said,
Each one... they had second thoughts,
As they stood there... with bowed head.

I looked to see that lonely man,
And he stared back at me,
His expression was a puzzled one,
It was plain for all to see.

He asked why I was merciful,
And why I cast no blame,
I told him... of a better man,
And that Jesus was his name.

I told him how he suffered,
How he died with a heavy heart,
How he was so good and kind to us,
Yet no—one took his part.

I looked once more at this poor man,
He stared... as if in trance,
I'm glad I never threw that stone,
And gave to him a chance.

For a chance is what we all need,
We've all sinned in some way... you see,
I hope that God is as merciful,
When they speak to him of me.

LONELINESS

Loneliness is a dreadful thing,
It's waiting and hoping for a doorbell to ring,
It means to sit from week to week,
To listen to silence... to hear each creak.

Loneliness is watching for the postman to call,
To watch him pass by... there's nothing at all,
The phone rings... to rouse any slumber,
A heart sinks... it's just a wrong number.

Loneliness is sitting by the fire each night,
To gaze at its embers... to picture a sight,
It means to have no company at all,
Just the shadows of flames... that flicker a wall.

Loneliness is cruel... so hard and unkind,
It plays many a trick on the weary mind,
Loneliness means that in life you are poor,
Your loved one no longer enters the door.

Loneliness is sitting and watching the clock,
Its pendulum swings... as it goes tick tock,
Loneliness crowds a mind with fear,
As that clock is all the sound you hear.

In loneliness... it seems like yesterday,
When this house was full of children at play,
At night we'd sit and play a game,
We always thought... 'twould stay the same.

Loneliness ... leaves no room for fun,
One starts to think of thing, undone,
To think this house was once a home,
It's now a shell... for the mind to roam.

Loneliness is a dreadful silence to one,
Who feels the end of life has begun,
It makes you wonder... where you went wrong,
Or where your friends and family have gone.

Loneliness is having not a single friend,
How does one cope... how does one tend,
You'll gaze at things on your mantel shelf,
You'll mutter and talk... but to yourself.

Loneliness can come at any stage,
It matters not what is your age,
If you have no-one to call at your home,
Young or old... your still alone.

Loneliness always unsettles the mind,
As answers to questions.. you try hard to find,
Why do my neighbours... all stay away,
Is it something I said... or didn't say.

Loneliness fills a heart with dread,
As you clutch your jar and trip to bed,
Before you sleep... you'll kneel and pray,
That perhaps to-morrow... is a better day.

PLEASE RETURN

Oh' God, please pay us a visit,
To see this world I'm in,
A world that's so unhappy,
And seems to thrive on sin.

To think that once you died for us,
To make our world sublime,
It seems by all our actions,
That you did waste your time.

When first you came to see us,
And no one knew your name,
People were mostly kind and good,
To-day it's not the same.

Our world is full of greed,
There's always a need for more,
No one seems to think to ask,
They'd rather go to war.

To see our youth would pain you,
For I know my heart it tugs,
To see young life so wasted,
By the use of drink and drugs.

Things have changed since you were here,
When you got the widow's mite,
To-day there's not much giving,
And few to notice plight.

We seem to forget your goodness,
How you were so good and kind,
And all those lessons you gave us,
I fear they've slipped our mind.

In my mind there is a thought... dear God,
And it fills my heart with pain,
To make this world a better place,
You'd have to die again.

There's little reason why you should,
For I see it at a glance,
We'd forget once more your sufferings,
How you gave to us our chance.

I feel I too must share the guilt,
Why our world is not the same,
For I fell to human weakness,
I must take my share of blame.

I hope you will forgive me,
As you hear the words I say,
You know what's in my heart,
As I kneel to you and pray.

You did the best you could for us,
On you there is no blame,
We must try... and do our best,
To honour your holy name.

THE LUCK OF FRIENDSHIP

Should your life be long or short,
Should your fortunes twist and bend,
You'll be so lucky in this life,
To have one to call a friend.

We'll know of many acquaintances,
But I was lucky you see,
As fortune it did deem to smile,
I enjoyed the friendship of three.

The first I knew as boy and youth,
My wish was his desire,
I could almost touch the closeness,
In the company... of Eddie Maguire.

We gave to each other so many things,
As through our youth we did roam,
But our friendship... was all too brief,
For Eddie was called to his home.

His passing it came as a shock to me,
It changed my outlook on life,
For Eddie was always a friend in deed,
And his friendship was ever so rife.

Never will I forget him,
I'll remember... as long as I live,
I oft do wonder... did I play my part,
What did I really give.

For friendship is not just receiving,
Sometimes it's put to the test,
Some people think a friend in need,
Is little more than a pest.

Yet this is where a friendship shines,
It's something that can't be bought,
It's something we give to each other,
And reward is something not sought.

I was glad to have my second friend,
In those dark days of my woe,
Patsy Sherry a friend... never left my side,
No matter wherever I'd go.

It's a friendship that's held up well,
And it will... as long as we live,
And yet once more I have to ask,
What is it... that I really give.

'Tis now I think of my third friend,
For repayment was never his game,
It was always a matter of giving,
Joe Sheehan my friend... is his name.

It took us a long time to meet,
We were both in our middle ages,
And yet our friendship gained in strength,
As it went through its various stages.

I don't know what he sees in me,
He smiles when he calls me Jim,
Again I ask... what do I give,
What do I do for him.

I've never seen him refuse a call,
When asked to do a good deed,
And there again... in our friendship,
I am always the one in need.

Sometimes I think he should chase me,
Yet he wont... as long as we live,
I've done so little... to deserve this friend,
Once more I ask... what do I give.

At least we all have one friend,
A friend who gives us his love,
He's a friend sometimes forgotten,
He is God... from those Heavens above.

THE FRAUD

One day I met a Palmist,
She took my hand to read,
I had to give her sixpence,
To perform this noted deed.

She told of many changes,
To come in to my life,
She said that I would marry,
And have a lovely wife.

She said my lifeline it was short,
That I shouldn't travel far,
'Twas then I took my sixpence back,
For that line was just a scar.

I try to imagine my descendants reading this poem
maybe two hundred years from now. It is now 1994.

DEAR DESCENDANTS

After I am dead and gone,
And have left this worldly stage,
I hope you'll enjoy... my caring thoughts,
As you turn and read each page.

To all my many descendants,
I hand you down this book,
Please give a thought to me,
As you turn each page and look.

Please don't forget my wife Kathleen,
The best a man could get,
I hope you have her loving ways,
You'd have loved her... if you'd met.

Let's hope we're both in Heaven,
For to bless and watch your home,
We'll both be very close to you,
As you sit and read a poem.

Even though you can't see us,
And there's little use to look,
Be sure we're both there smiling,
As you gaze upon this book.

We're sorry we couldn't meet you all,
But life doesn't work that way,
You'll just have to read my poems,
They'll tell you... what I had to say.

Don't read this poem with sadness,
For we both had a wonderful life,
We both had our share of happiness,
With that usual mixture of strife.

Should you ever try to trace us,
Just look up the family tree,
And there on a swaying branch,
You'll find dear Kathleen and me.

She proudly bore the name of McGuigan,
But then on September's tenth day,
She stood at my side... she became my bride,
And changed her name to Wray.

We had two sons in Jim and John,
We raised them in good cheer,
We're glad of course we had them,
Otherwise you wouldn't be here.

Both of us wish you happiness,
No matter wherever you roam,
And should you feel... a little sad,
From this book... just read out a poem.

WRITING

I love to write about the things,
That helped to shape my life,
I write about my place of work,
And I write about my wife.

I write about the happy times,
When goodness seemed so rife,
I write too of the sad times,
When I had to see out strife.

I love to write about old friends,
Some of them long gone,
How they slowly seemed to drift,
As they went off... one by one.

I have written of my childhood days,
When I never had a care,
Or of the time I faced a world,
Whose rules they seemed unfair.

I write too of my family life,
In their midst I felt secure,
They made my life seem all worthwhile,
Of that I feel so sure.

I write about the religious life,
And I also write of love,
I write about our own dear God,
As he guides us from above.

Yet most of life is happiness,
And I write to tell you why,
I have my faith, and I have my health,
And I'll have them till I die.